GOLD MEDAL GAMES

Pictures, Puzzles, Facts, and Fun for Kids Ages 6–9

Written by Pamela Amick Klawitter, Ed.D. and Sherri Butterfield
Illustrated by Beverly Armstrong

The Learning Works

Cover Design & Illustration:
Bev Armstrong

Editing and Typography:
Kimberley A. Clark

Copyright © 1996
The Learning Works, Inc.
P.O. Box 6187
Santa Barbara, California 93160

ISBN: 0-88160-255-8

Contents

Introduction

Gold Medal Games is a collection of pictures and puzzles, facts and fun—all based on the Olympic tradition, both ancient and modern. Written for primary-aged children, it tells the story of these "games for gold" and names the sports events they include. This book contains

- hidden words to be searched for
- hidden objects to be found
- dots to be connected
- illustrations to be colored
- mazes to be traced
- pictures to be identified
- puzzles to be solved
- things to be designed
- interesting facts and stories
- an answer key on page 64

The activities in this book are ideal for use at home, in the classroom, or while traveling.

For children who are ready for a more comprehensive Olympic adventure, look into *Victory,* written by Karen Dick and Diane Sylvester and also published by The Learning Works.

The First Olympic Games

The Olympic Games started more than three thousand years ago in a distant country called Greece. The earliest Olympics were part of a religious festival which lasted for several days and ended with a victory banquet. At first, the only sporting event was a footrace.

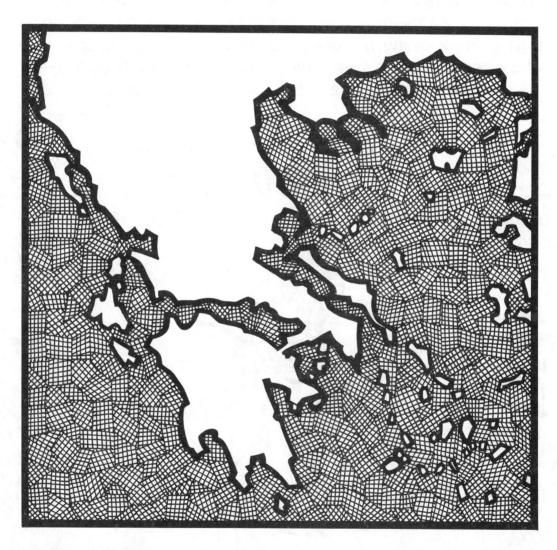

A Special Prize

These early Olympics took place every four years. They were held in a meadow at the foot of Mount Olympus. The Greeks built special buildings to hold the events. Almost three hundred Olympic festivals were held at this location. As the games became more popular, different sporting events were added. Men came from all over Greece to take part in events such as running, wrestling, boxing, horse racing, and chariot racing. The winner of each event was given a crown of olive leaves. Sometimes he was also given another prize. Connect the dots to find out what it was.

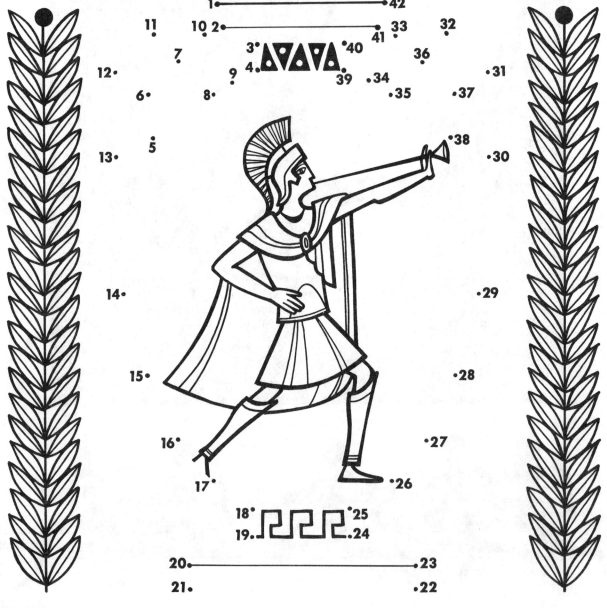

Find the Hidden Woman

For many years, the Greeks would not let women take part in these games. They would not even let women watch. One runner's mother, who had helped her son train, dressed herself as a man so that she could see her son race. In the picture below, she is hiding in a fruit tree as she watches him run. To find her, color only those clumps of leaves that have a piece of fruit in them.

Women in the Olympics

Until 1896, only men took part in the Games but, in 1900, a few events for women were added. Since then, more and more women have competed at each new Olympics. Today, women compete in most of the sports.

The Chariot Races

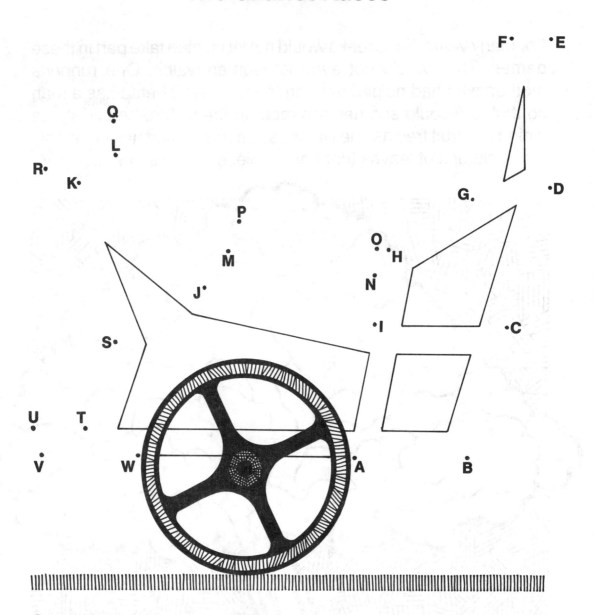

One of the most popular events was the chariot race. In this six-mile race, a driver rode in a small two-wheeled cart pulled by four horses. Sometimes forty or more chariots gathered on the track to compete in the twelve-lap race. Because the track was so crowded, many accidents happened. Often, only one or two chariots would finish the race.

This was one of the first types of races that women were allowed to take part in. At first they could only train the horses and hire a driver. Later, women actually drove the chariots. Connect the dots in the picture above to discover what a chariot looked like.

Olympic Footraces

Also popular in the early Olympics were the footraces. There were several types. In the longest race, runners ran twenty-four lengths of the stadium field. A shorter race was only two lengths of the stadium. The fastest race, or sprint, was one stadium length.

There was even a special race for soldiers dressed in armor and carrying their heavy swords and shields. Runners did a lot of pushing and shoving, so many people got hurt in these races.

The End of the Olympic Games

THEODOSIUS

The Greek Olympics took place for many years. They even continued after soldiers from Rome, a powerful city in Italy, won a war with Greece. After that, Roman emperors ruled Greece. Even though the Games lasted under Roman rule, the spirit behind them changed. Olympic athletes began to compete for money instead of olive branches. Eventually, an emperor named Theodosius decided to end the Olympic Games. By then, the Olympics had lasted about 1,200 years. Over time, the buildings and walls around the Olympic fields were torn down or destroyed by earthquakes, landslides, and floods.

Baron Pierre de Coubertin

For more than a thousand years there were no Olympic Games. Then, someone found the ruins of the old stadium at Olympia. A Frenchman visited these ruins and got the idea of starting the games again. This man was a teacher whose name was Baron Pierre de Coubertin. He wanted young people all over the world to understand each other better. He thought that a modern Olympics would be the best way to bring young athletes from many countries together.

Olympic Word Search

At last, Pierre de Coubertin's dream came true. After much hard work, the first modern Olympic Games were finally held in 1896 in Athens, Greece. Thirteen countries participated with athletes from ten of them winning medals. The winning countries were Australia, Austria, Denmark, England, France, Germany, Greece, Hungary, Switzerland, and the United States.

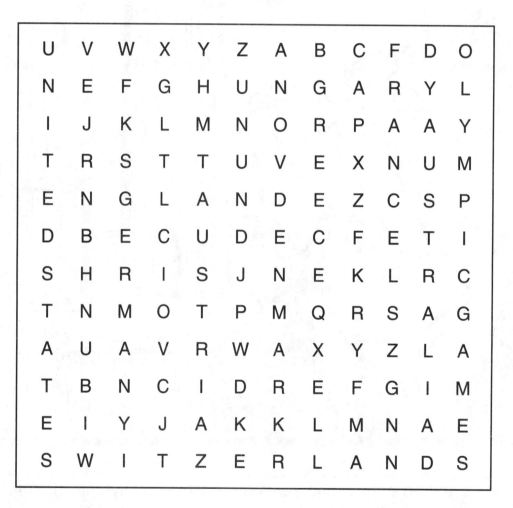

U	V	W	X	Y	Z	A	B	C	F	D	O
N	E	F	G	H	U	N	G	A	R	Y	L
I	J	K	L	M	N	O	R	P	A	A	Y
T	R	S	T	T	U	V	E	X	N	U	M
E	N	G	L	A	N	D	E	Z	C	S	P
D	B	E	C	U	D	E	C	F	E	T	I
S	H	R	I	S	J	N	E	K	L	R	C
T	N	M	O	T	P	M	Q	R	S	A	G
A	U	A	V	R	W	A	X	Y	Z	L	A
T	B	N	C	I	D	R	E	F	G	I	M
E	I	Y	J	A	K	K	L	M	N	A	E
S	W	I	T	Z	E	R	L	A	N	D	S

Look at the letters in the box above. Find and circle the names of the ten countries that won medals in the first modern Olympic Games. Then look for two bonus words. Remember to look from left to right and from top to bottom.

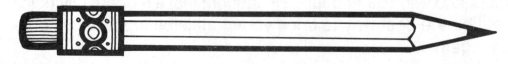

Olympic Events

Almost three hundred athletes came to the first Olympics to take part in nine different sporting events—cycling, fencing, gymnastics, shooting, swimming, tennis, track and field, weight lifting, and wrestling. Find each of these nine Olympic events in the pictures above.

Early Marathons

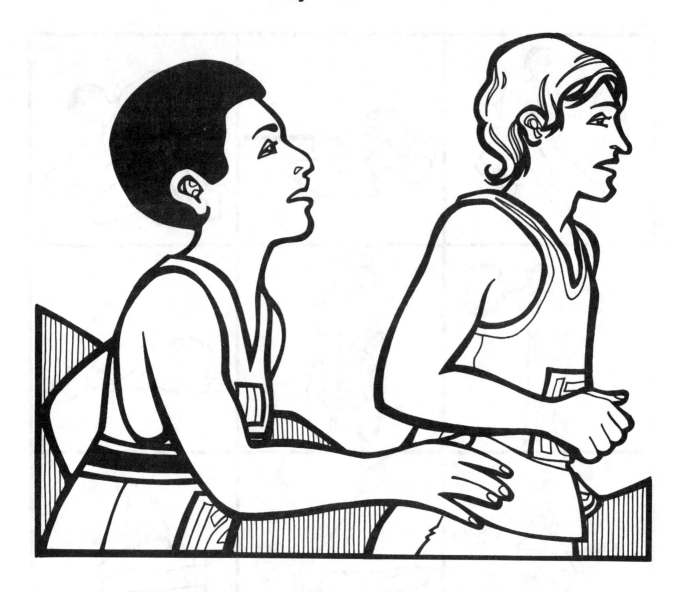

An important event in the 1896 Olympics was the marathon. This long and difficult footrace showed how hard an Olympic athlete needed to work to succeed. This race was about twenty-six miles long. Thousands of people stood along the roads of the race course and crowded into the stadium to watch the finish. Twenty-five runners began the race, but many did not make it to the end.

The race was finally won by a Greek runner named Spiridon Loues. The crowd was very excited. The King of Greece was in the audience. He waved his hat in the air for so long that he tore off the brim.

The International Olympic Committee

Before the 1896 Olympics, a group of people got together to organize the games. They formed the International Olympic Committee, or the IOC. It would be their job to make the rules for future Olympics.

For each Olympics, the IOC chooses which sports will be included and which country will host the Games. For a sport to be included in the Olympics, it must be popular in many countries.

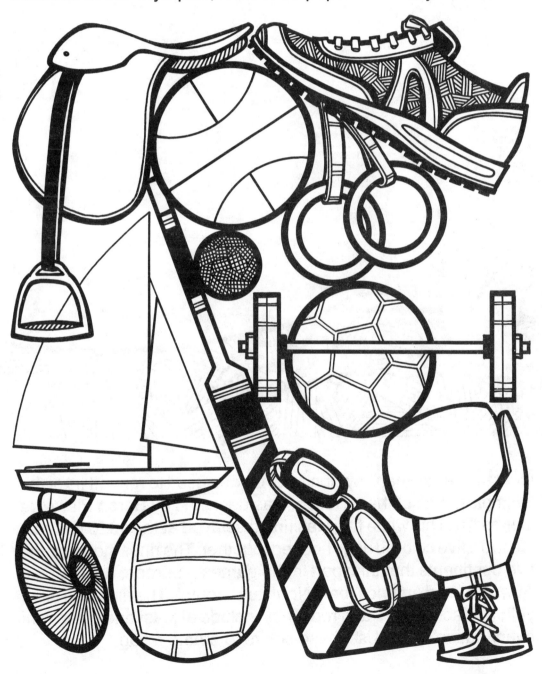

Design a Flag

Over the years, many symbols have been used to remind us of the Olympics. One of these, a flag, was designed by Baron Pierre de Coubertin. This white flag was first displayed at the 1920 Games. On it are five colored rings hooked together. The rings stand for the five continents that take part in the games—Europe, Asia, Africa, Australia, and America (both North and South). The rings are blue, yellow, black, green, and red. They include at least one color from every nation's flag. Use these colors to create a flag.

Create an Olympic Stamp

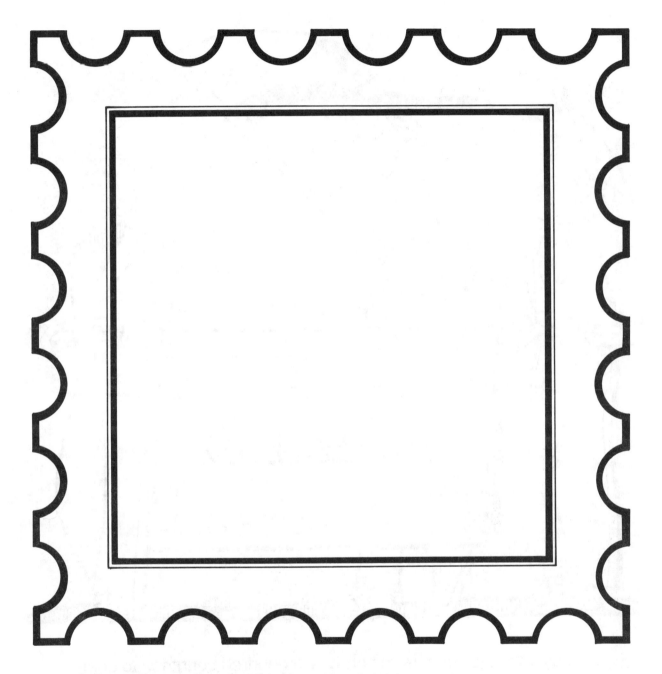

Artists all over the world create special things to help people enjoy and remember the Olympic Games. For the first modern Olympics in 1896, a set of postage stamps was designed and sold to help pay the cost of putting on the Games. In the space above, design a postage stamp for a future Olympics. Remember to include a picture, the name of your country, and the amount of money the stamp is worth.

The Opening Ceremony

Today, athletes come from nearly two hundred countries to compete in the Summer Olympic Games. Together, they take part in the Parade of Nations during the Opening Ceremony before the Games begin. Groups of athletes from each country march into the stadium wearing colorful costumes. In honor of the first Olympics, the Greek athletes always enter the stadium first. The other countries march into the stadium in alphabetical order. Athletes from the host country enter last.

The Olympic Flame

Another part of the Opening Ceremony is the lighting of the Olympic Flame. This tradition began in ancient Greece. In 1936, the custom started again and has been carried on ever since. Four weeks before the Olympics begin, Olympic officials meet in Greece. They have a ceremony to light the Olympic Flame at the site of the ancient Olympics.

This flame is passed from torch to torch and runner to runner. It travels all the way from Greece to the host city for the Olympics. Sometimes the flame travels by plane as it crosses oceans or mountains. The last runner enters the stadium during the Opening Ceremony and uses the burning torch to light a flame, which will burn throughout the Games.

Create an Olympic Mascot

Sometimes a mascot is designed for the Olympic Games. In 1980, it was Misha the Bear, and in 1984, it was Sam the Olympic Eagle. The 1996 mascot for the Atlanta Olympics is called Whatizit. It was first shown at the Closing Ceremony of the 1992 Olympics in Barcelona, Spain. Later, Whatizit was shortened to "IZZY" when children around the world were asked to suggest a name.

IZZY is a colorful, animated character with huge sneakers, starry eyes, a big smile, and lightning bolt eyebrows. He is decorated with Olympic rings and carries an Olympic Torch. IZZY can magically change size and shape to take part in all Olympic sports.

Use your imagination to create a mascot for a future Olympics. Draw and color your mascot in the box above.

Olympic Pictograms

Pictograms are simple drawings that send messages with pictures instead of words. Pictograms have been used in the Olympics since 1948. They can be understood by people from any country who visit the Olympics. Each pictogram stands for a different sport.

Thirty pictograms designed for the 1996 Olympics in Atlanta show athletes in action to illustrate the sports. These pictures are displayed on signs, programs, and products throughout the Olympics to publicize the official sporting events.

An example of a pictogram is shown above. It might be used for the track and field events.

Fifteen pictograms are shown on the next page. On the line beneath each pictogram, place the name of the sport that is pictured. Choose from the sports that are listed below.

archery	cycling	judo
baseball	diving	swimming
basketball	fencing	tennis
boxing	gymnastics	volleyball
canoeing	hockey	weight lifting

Pictogram Match

_____ _____ _____

_____ _____ _____

_____ _____ _____

_____ _____ _____

_____ _____ _____

Design an Olympic Medal

All athletes who compete in the Olympics receive a commemorative medal. The first-, second-, and third-place winners are given special medals to wear around their necks. The first-place medal is gold, the second-place medal is silver, and the third-place medal is bronze. The design for the Olympic medal was created in 1928 by Italian artist Giuseppe Cassioli. Since 1972, Cassioli's design has been used on the front of the medal, and the host city's design is used on the back of the medal. In the space below, create a design for the back side which would be appropriate for the next Olympic Games, either summer or winter.

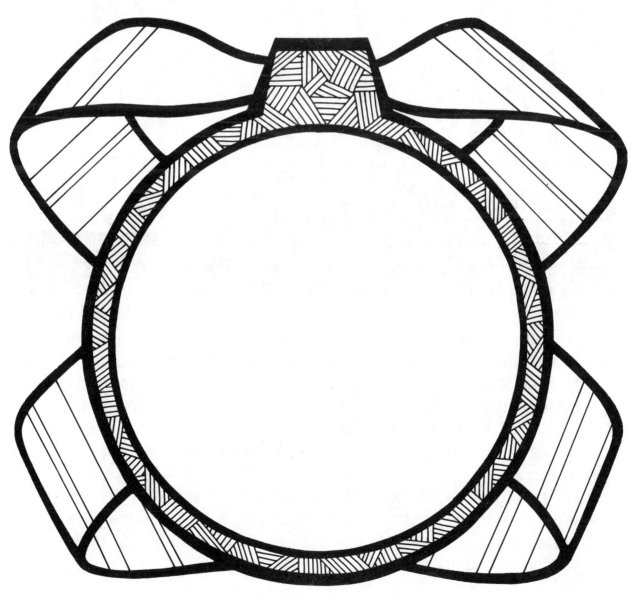

Announcing the Winners

Medals are awarded to the winners at a special Victory Ceremony at the end of each event. The first-, second-, and third-place finishers step up onto a special awards platform. The platform has three different levels. The first-place winner stands in the middle on the highest level. The runner-up stands a little lower to the winner's right and the third-place finisher stands on the lowest level to the winner's left.

The flag from each medalist's country is flown over the platform, with the winner's flag in the highest position. After the medals are placed around the athletes' necks, the national anthem of the gold medalist's country is played.

The Closing Ceremony

The end of the Olympics is marked with a special Closing Ceremony. Once again, everyone gathers at the Olympic Stadium. The athletes parade into the stadium. This time, they do not come in country by country. Instead, they enter in a large group to show friendship.

The national anthem of Greece is played as the athletes enter the stadium. In addition to the Olympic flag, three other flags are displayed. The host country's flag flies in the center, with the flag of Greece to its right and the flag of the host country for the next Olympics to its left.

In a special Olympic flag exchange, the mayor of the host city presents the flag to the mayor of the host city for the next Olympics. The Olympic Games are declared closed and the Olympic Flame is put out.

The Summer Olympics

The IOC decided that the modern Olympic Games would be held during the summer every four years. This remained the schedule until 1924, when the Winter Olympics were added.

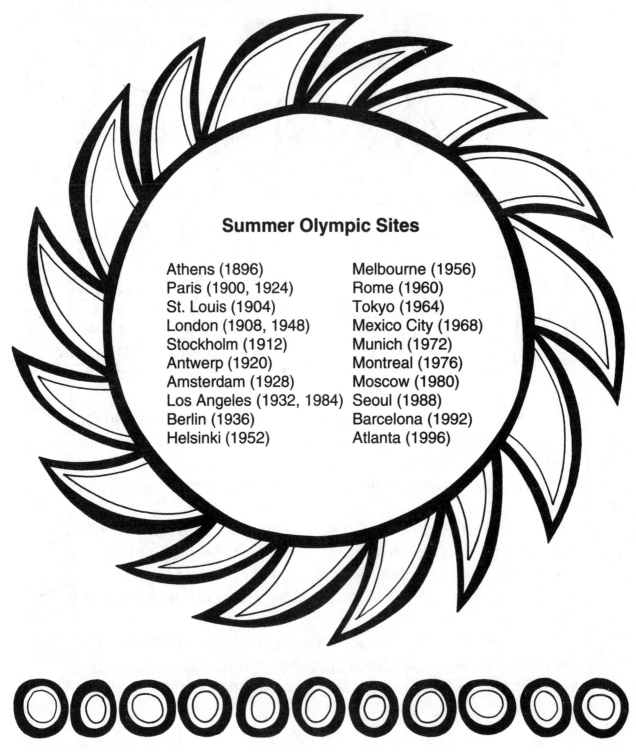

Summer Olympic Sites

Athens (1896)
Paris (1900, 1924)
St. Louis (1904)
London (1908, 1948)
Stockholm (1912)
Antwerp (1920)
Amsterdam (1928)
Los Angeles (1932, 1984)
Berlin (1936)
Helsinki (1952)

Melbourne (1956)
Rome (1960)
Tokyo (1964)
Mexico City (1968)
Munich (1972)
Montreal (1976)
Moscow (1980)
Seoul (1988)
Barcelona (1992)
Atlanta (1996)

New Olympic Events

Athletes compete in many different Olympic sports. The number and type of events change from one Olympics to the next. Sports that are no longer popular are dropped and newer, more popular ones are added. The 1996 Olympics in Atlanta, Georgia, added several new sports, including men's and women's beach volleyball and mountain bike racing, as well as women's softball and soccer. Draw a picture of one of these new Olympic events.

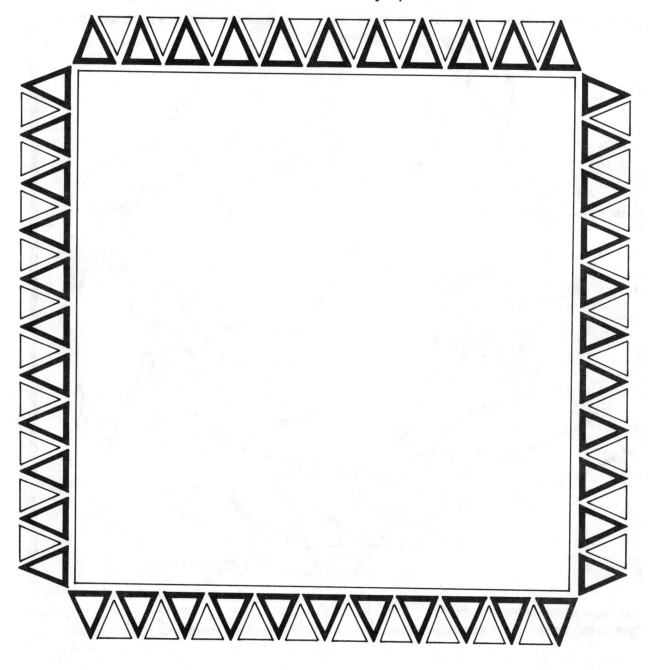

Events of the Summer Olympics

At the Summer Olympics, athletes compete in track and field events, water sports, and gymnastics. Team sports such as soccer, basketball, and volleyball are also played. There are individual sports such as archery, boxing, cycling, fencing, horseback riding, judo, shooting, table tennis, tennis, wrestling, and weight lifting.

Track and Field Events

In the modern Olympics, as in the Olympics in ancient Greece, track and field events are very popular. Track and field events include jumping events, throwing events, and running events. Running events cover distances from one hundred meters to the marathon, which is just over twenty-six miles long. The short races, called sprints, are exciting to watch. The long-distance races, especially the marathon, require runners to pace themselves over a long period of time.

Jumping Events

Hurdles and steeplechase are track and field events in which runners must go over or through different obstacles. For example, the men's steeplechase race involves jumping over hurdles, small bushes, and pools of water.

Several types of jumping events are held, including the long jump, the high jump, and the triple jump. The pole vault is a special event where jumpers use a long, flexible pole to help them get over a high bar. This event is for men only.

Throwing Events

Track and field also includes throwing events—the discus throw, the hammer throw, the javelin throw, and the shot put. Pictured in the boxes below are the objects that are thrown in these four events. Match each of these objects with its Olympic throwing event. Write the name of the event on the line below the object.

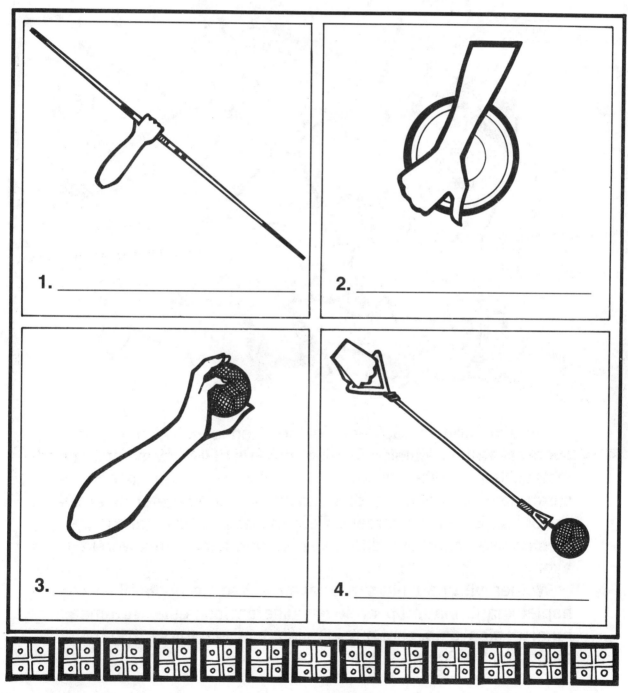

1. _____

2. _____

3. _____

4. _____

The Decathlon and Heptathlon

All-around ability in track and field for men is tested in a special event called the decathlon. The decathlon is a two-day event which tests skills in ten different areas. Each athlete takes part in the 100-meter dash, long jump, shot put, high jump, 400-meter run, 110-meter hurdles, discus throw, pole vault, javelin throw, and 1,500-meter run. Winners are determined by the total points won in all events.

Women take part in a similar event called the heptathlon. The heptathlon is made up of seven different contests: 100-meter hurdles, high jump, shot put, long jump, javelin throw, 200-meter dash, and the 800-meter dash.

Water Events

Many types of water sports also take place. There are individual swimming races of different lengths using strokes such as the backstroke, the breast stroke, or the butterfly. There are also relay races that involve more than one swimmer. Other popular water sports are platform and springboard diving, and water polo. The number of swimming events has grown from only four in the 1896 Olympics to over thirty in the 1996 Olympics.

One unique water sport is synchronized swimming for women. This used to be called water ballet because swimmers make patterns in the water to music, as if dancing. These swimmers must hold their breath for more than thirty seconds under the water while judges watch them with the aid of underwater cameras.

Water Races

There are several types of boat races in the Olympics. Each uses a different type of paddle or oar. In kayak racing, a paddle with a blade on each end is used. The racer holds the paddle in the middle and takes turns dipping one end and then the other on opposite sides of the kayak.

In Canadian canoe racing, the paddle has a blade on only one end. The racer kneels in the center of the canoe and switches the blade from one side to the other. There are two types of kayak and canoe races—flatwater sprints and whitewater slalom races where racers must go around buoys and markers in the water. Rowing races are also part of the Olympics. The boats used in these races are long and narrow. They are called shells or sculls. One, two, or four rowers, each using two long oars, pull the boat quickly across the water. Can you identify the three types of boats pictured?

Gymnastic Events

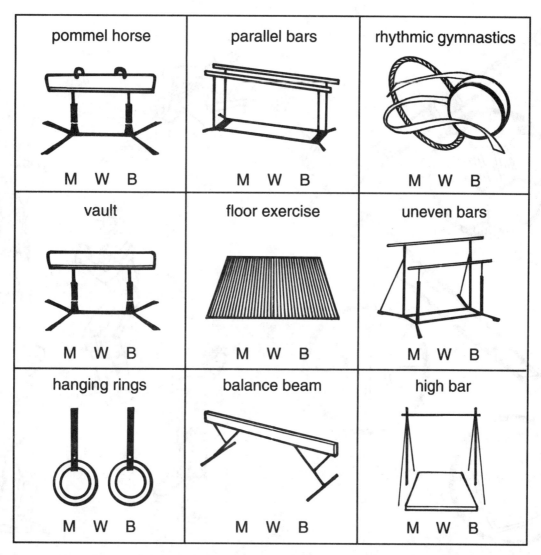

Gymnastics has always been part of the modern Olympics. Women gymnasts compete in five events—balance beam, floor exercise, uneven bars, vault, and rhythmic gymnastics. Rhythmic gymnasts use hoops, balls, clubs, and a long satin ribbon while doing dance movements to music.

Men compete in six events—floor exercise, hanging rings, high bar, parallel bars, vault, and side horse, which is sometimes called the pommel horse. It is like the vault, except that it has two handles.

Look at the equipment shown above. Would it be used by men, women, or both? Under each picture circle M if it is used only by men, W if it is used only by women, or B if it is used by both men and women.

Team Events

Team sports are another exciting part of the Olympics. Football, or soccer (as it is called in North America), was the first team sport in the Olympics. Another team sport, field hockey, is played much like soccer. Players don't kick the ball; they hit it into the goal with big flat sticks.

Basketball was first played in the 1936 Olympics. The first games were held outdoors, not indoors like today's games. U.S. teams have always done well in this sport. Volleyball was not played in the Olympics until 1964. Baseball became an Olympic sport in 1992. Draw a line from each item on the left to the athlete on the right who uses it.

Individual Sports

Here are some Summer Olympic sports at a glance.

Archery

A bow is used to shoot arrows at a target. Each archer shoots 144 arrows at targets that are different distances away. Points are earned for accuracy.

Boxing

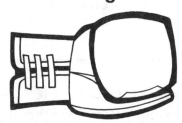

Boxing is for men only. Two men go into the boxing ring and fight three two-minute rounds. At the end of each round, points are given to the fighters by five judges. These points are for fighting style, not strength. Boxers wear padded leather gloves and protective head gear.

Cycling

Cycling events include both track racing and road racing. Track races are held on a special oval indoor track called a velodrome. Road races are long distance races held outdoors.

Fencing

In fencing, a player scores points by touching his or her opponent with the tip of a thin sword. The players are protected by masks and special clothing. A fenching contest, or *match,* is held on a long, narrow court called a *strip.*

Individual Sports
(continued)

Horseback Riding

One riding, or equestrian, event is show jumping where the rider guides the horse twice around a course which has twelve to fifteen different jumps. Another event is dressage, which tests how well the horse will obey the rider's commands to walk, trot, canter, and change direction. Another three-day event includes jumping, dressage, and a test of endurance where the rider guides the horse through a long-distance obstacle run.

Judo

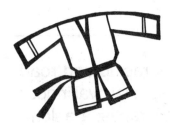

Judo is a sport that originated in Japan. Two athletes fight hand-to-hand. To win, one fighter must hold the other down, or get him in an arm lock or choke hold. After five minutes, if neither athlete has won the match, the fighter with the most points is declared the winner.

Shooting

Since 1896, many types of shooting events have been part of the Olympics. Today, pistol and rifle shooting at both still and moving targets are popular. Trap shooting, or skeet shooting, is an event where a clay saucer called a "pigeon" is thrown into the air and the shooter is allowed two shots to try to hit it. Women first competed in shooting events in 1984.

Individual Sports
(continued)

Table Tennis

Another name for table tennis is ping-pong. Players hit a small, hollow, plastic ball back and forth across a net on a special table. The ball is often hit at speeds of over one hundred miles per hour. Players must have very quick reflexes.

Weight Lifting

This sport tests an athlete's body strength. He must lift a heavy, weighted bar over his head in two different ways. In the "snatch" he must use both hands to lift the bar from the floor over his head in one smooth motion. In the "clean and jerk" the bar is lifted overhead in two motions. First the bar is lifted to the chest, and then overhead. An athlete gets three tries at each type of lift. The winner in each weight class is the man who lifts the heaviest total weight in both events combined.

Wrestling

Wrestling has been popular since the early Greek Olympics. Wrestlers in the same weight class compete two at a time and one man gets points for holding or pinning the other to the ground, keeping him under control, or escaping his hold. There are two types of wrestling. In freestyle, the wrestler may use hands, arms, or legs and can hold his opponent above or below the waist. In Greco-Roman, the wrestler can't hold with his legs, trip his opponent, or hold him below the waist.

Read to find out more about these and other Summer Olympic sports.

Summer Sports Match

Place the letter from the description on the right
that matches each sport on the left.

1. _____ archery

2. _____ badminton

3. _____ boxing

4. _____ decathlon

5. _____ football

6. _____ gymnastics

7. _____ marathon

8. _____ synchronized swimming

9. _____ table tennis

10. _____ wrestling

a. Another name for this sport is water ballet.

b. A "shuttlecock" or bird is used in this sport.

c. This race is about twenty-six miles long.

d. This is sometimes called ping-pong.

e. In North America, this game is called soccer.

f. Uneven bars and a balance beam are used in this sport.

g. One way to win a match is to pin your opponent.

h. Padded leather gloves are needed for this sport.

i. A bow and arrow are used in this sport.

j. Ten different events make up this sport.

Hidden Treasures

Can you find a way to hide each piece of sports equipment in a picture of your own? Draw details and color your picture. An example is started for you to finish.

U.S. Medals in Ten Summer Olympics

Year	Gold Medals	Silver Medals	Bronze Medals
1952	40	19	17
1956	32	25	17
1960	34	21	16
1964	36	26	28
1968	45	28	34
1972	33	31	30
1976	34	35	25
1984	83	61	30
1988	36	31	27
1992	37	34	37

Use the information in the chart above
to help you answer the following questions.

1. In which year did the U.S. win the fewest gold medals? _____

2. How many medals did the U.S. win altogether in 1972? _____

3. In which year did the U.S. win more silver medals than gold? _____

4. In which three years did the U.S. win more bronze medals than silver medals? _____, _____, and _____

5. In which year did the U.S. win the same number of gold and bronze medals? _____

The First Winter Olympics

The Summer Olympics are many centuries old, but the Winter Olympics are relatively new. They were started in this century. When the French hosted the Summer Olympics in 1924, they decided to hold a week of winter sporting events. The International Olympic Committee liked the idea and voted to call these events the Winter Olympic Games.

They would be held every four years. At first they were held in the same year as the Summer Olympics. Since 1992, the Winter and Summer Games have been held two years apart so that the world can enjoy Olympic Games more often.

Winter Olympic Sites

1924	Chamonix, France
1928	St. Moritz, Switzerland
1932	Lake Placid, New York, U.S.A.
1936	Garmisch-Partenkirchen, Germany
1948	St. Moritz, Switzerland
1952	Oslo, Norway
1956	Cortina d'Ampezzo, Italy
1960	Squaw Valley, California, U.S.A.
1964	Innsbruck, Austria
1968	Grenoble, France
1972	Sapporo, Japan
1976	Innsbruck, Austria
1980	Lake Placid, New York, U.S.A.
1984	Sarajevo, Yugoslavia
1988	Calgary, Canada
1992	Albertville, France
1994	Lillehammer, Norway
1998	Nagano, Japan

Mogul Maze

A new event first held at the 1992 Olympics was freestyle mogul skiing. Moguls are bumps made on the ski slope with snow-grooming machines. Skiers must make high-speed turns over and between the moguls as they race down the slope. They must also do two acrobatic moves as they come down the hill. Help this skier find a path down the hill over and between the moguls. Trace the path with your pencil.

FINISH

Cross-Country Races and Ski Jumping

Two Nordic ski events are cross-country races and ski jumping. Cross-country races are long-distance races across snowy fields and through the woods. The skis in this event are longer and thinner than downhill skis. In ski jumping, the skiers ski down a steep ramp covered with snow and sail through the air for long distances before landing on the ground. Each skier jumps two times and is judged on the distance jumped and the style of the jump and the landing. Skis for jumping are longer and heavier than downhill skis.

Speed Skating and Figure Skating

Speed skating events are held on an oval, ice-covered track. Both indoor and outdoor tracks are used. Skaters race two at a time around the track. One skater starts on the shorter, inside lane, and the other starts on the longer, outside lane. Each time around the track, they change lanes. They are racing against the clock. To help them race faster, they wear very tight clothing and skates with long, sharp blades.

There are three types of figure skating events—individual, pairs, and ice dancing. Skaters must be both strong and graceful. In pair skating and ice dancing, a man and woman skate together as a team. In all three events, skating programs are performed to music. There is a short program where skaters must perform certain moves. There is also a longer freestyle program in which skaters make up their own moves.

Ice Hockey and Bobsled/Luge Racing

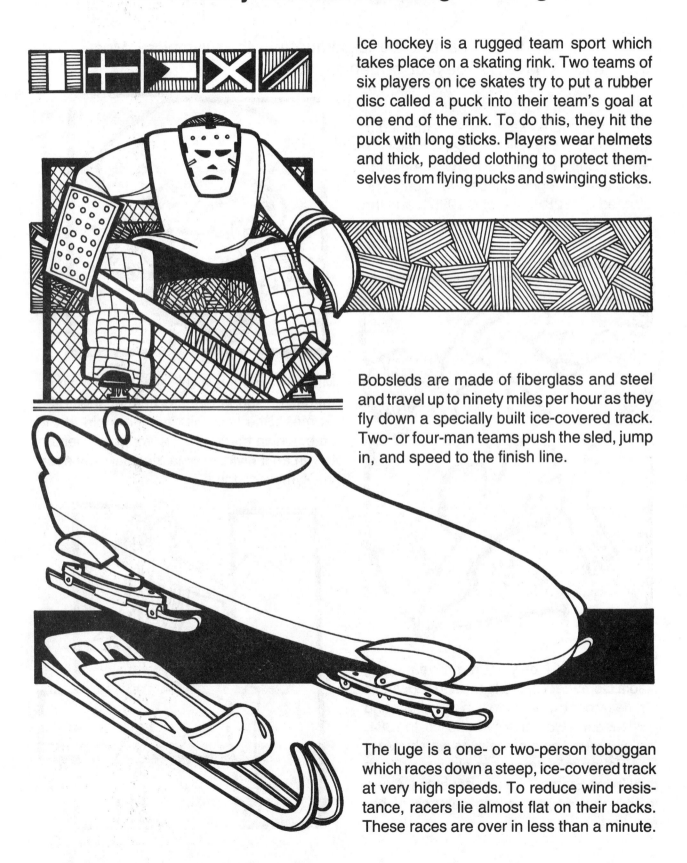

Ice hockey is a rugged team sport which takes place on a skating rink. Two teams of six players on ice skates try to put a rubber disc called a puck into their team's goal at one end of the rink. To do this, they hit the puck with long sticks. Players wear helmets and thick, padded clothing to protect themselves from flying pucks and swinging sticks.

Bobsleds are made of fiberglass and steel and travel up to ninety miles per hour as they fly down a specially built ice-covered track. Two- or four-man teams push the sled, jump in, and speed to the finish line.

The luge is a one- or two-person toboggan which races down a steep, ice-covered track at very high speeds. To reduce wind resistance, racers lie almost flat on their backs. These races are over in less than a minute.

Young Athletes

How old do you have to be to compete in the Olympics? Most events have no age requirements.

One of the figure skaters who competed in the first Winter Olympics in 1924 was eleven-year-old Sonja Henie from Norway. Although she came in eighth place that year, she returned in 1928, 1932, and 1936 to win the gold medal each time!

Marjorie Gestring, a U.S. diver, won the gold medal in springboard diving at the 1936 Games. She was thirteen years old at the time, which made her the youngest person to win an individual gold medal in any sport in Olympic history!

When she was only fourteen years old, Nadia Comaneci came to the 1976 Olympic Games from Romania to win the all-around gold medal in women's gymnastics. In 1984, the all-around gold medal was won by Mary Lou Retton, a sixteen-year-old athlete from the United States. She had never taken part in an important international competition before that!

Young Athletes

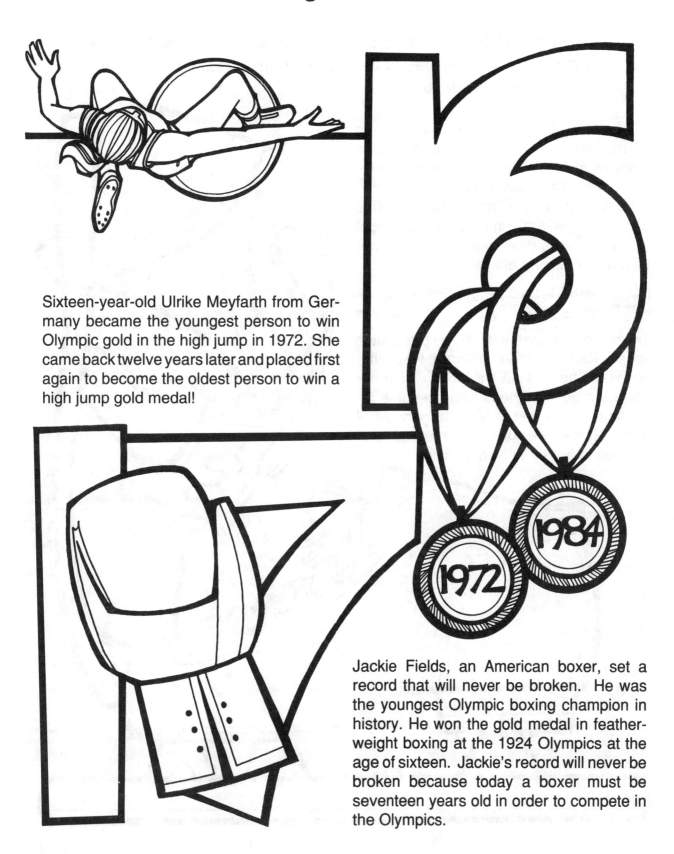

Sixteen-year-old Ulrike Meyfarth from Germany became the youngest person to win Olympic gold in the high jump in 1972. She came back twelve years later and placed first again to become the oldest person to win a high jump gold medal!

Jackie Fields, an American boxer, set a record that will never be broken. He was the youngest Olympic boxing champion in history. He won the gold medal in featherweight boxing at the 1924 Olympics at the age of sixteen. Jackie's record will never be broken because today a boxer must be seventeen years old in order to compete in the Olympics.

The Road to Success

The road to Olympic success is not always an easy one to follow. Some athletes have had to overcome many obstacles in order to accomplish their dreams.

After winning a gold medal in track at the age of 16, American Betty Robinson was in a plane crash which left her unable to walk for two years. She regained the use of her legs, but couldn't bend her knee completely. This didn't stop her from running, however. Eight years later, she came back to win another gold medal as part of a relay team.

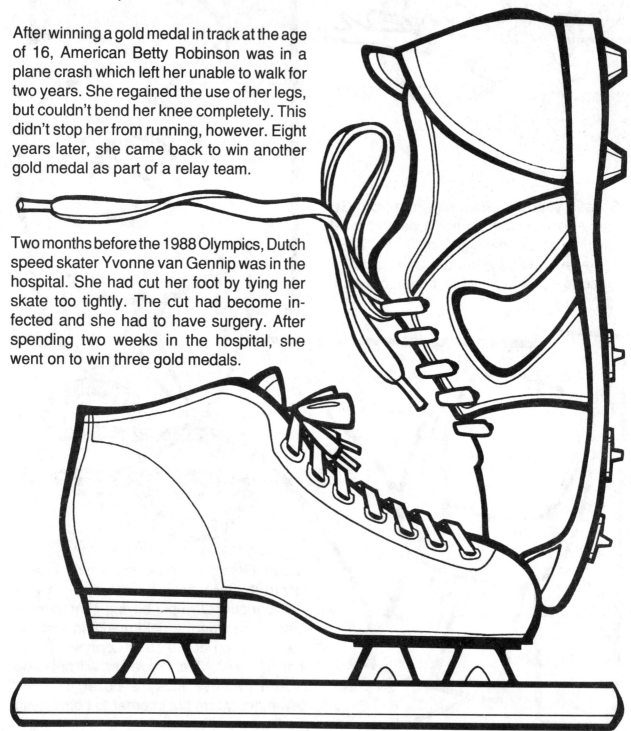

Two months before the 1988 Olympics, Dutch speed skater Yvonne van Gennip was in the hospital. She had cut her foot by tying her skate too tightly. The cut had become infected and she had to have surgery. After spending two weeks in the hospital, she went on to win three gold medals.

The Road to Success

Bill Smith was very sick as a small child. When he was six years old, he had a disease called typhoid fever. He took up swimming to help make himself stronger. At the 1948 Olympics, he won a gold medal for the U.S. in swimming.

Wilma Rudolph, a U.S. track star, had twenty-one brothers and sisters. She weighed only 4.5 pounds when she was born and was very sick as a child. She had polio, scarlet fever, and pneumonia. She could not use her left leg and had to wear a brace on it. She worked hard all through her childhood to learn to walk and then to run without her brace. By the time she turned sixteen, she qualified for the U.S. Olympic track team. She went on to win three gold medals at the 1960 Olympics.

Interview a family member or friend about an obstacle he or she has faced and overcome. Neatly copy your interview or story onto a clean piece of paper. Add a photo or drawing of the person and share your finished work with the person you interviewed.

What's My Job?

Who are the Olympic athletes? Believe it or not, athletes come from all walks of life. Did you know that . . .

an American FBI agent won a gold medal in track and field in the 1952 Olympics?

in 1956, a wood chopper from Sweden won a speed skating gold medal?

a carpenter from Yugoslavia won a gold medal in canoeing in 1976?

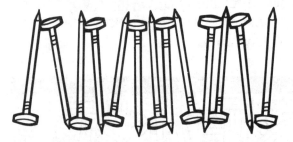

a policeman from Poland boxed his way to a gold medal in 1968?

a doctor won the gold medal and an engineer won the silver medal in fencing in 1972?

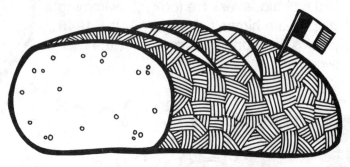

a bakery delivery man from France won the gold medal in the 1900 marathon?

a former deep-sea diver from the Soviet Union won a weight lifting gold medal in the 1956 Olympic games?

an American guitar player won a gold medal in boxing in 1976?

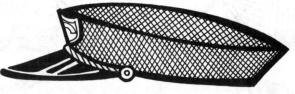

a mechanic from Italy became a gold medal winner in cycling in the 1964 Olympic Games?

What a Disaster!

For most athletes, the Olympics is the most exciting time in their lives. But, sometimes things go wrong! That's exactly what happened to these unlucky athletes. Here are their stories.

The soccer team from Spain was a favorite in the 1924 Olympics in France. In the last minute of the game, one of the players kicked the ball past his own goalkeeper to score the winning goal for the other team!

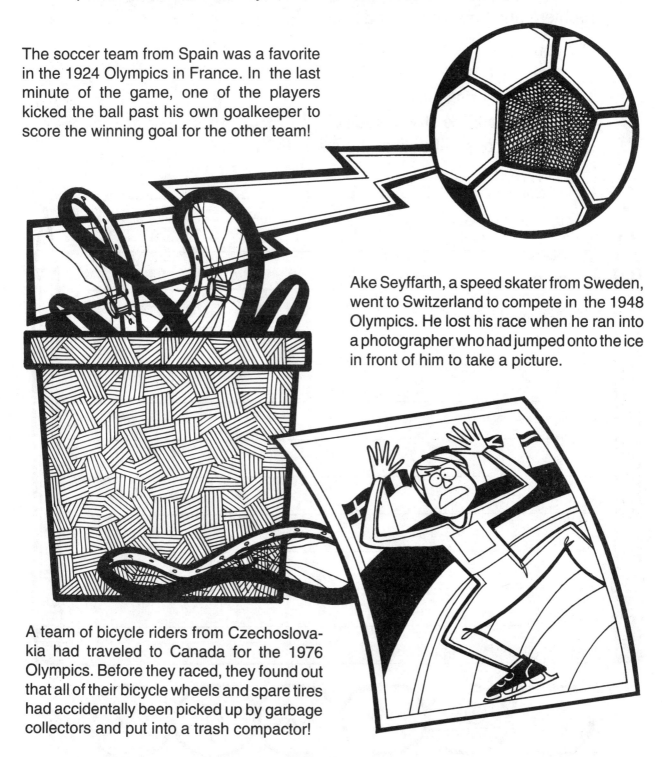

Ake Seyffarth, a speed skater from Sweden, went to Switzerland to compete in the 1948 Olympics. He lost his race when he ran into a photographer who had jumped onto the ice in front of him to take a picture.

A team of bicycle riders from Czechoslovakia had traveled to Canada for the 1976 Olympics. Before they raced, they found out that all of their bicycle wheels and spare tires had accidentally been picked up by garbage collectors and put into a trash compactor!

Diary of My Disaster

It is the biggest day of your life! You are ready to compete in the Olympics. Everything is perfect. Your event is about to begin. Suddenly, something goes wrong. Write a short story about your problem and how you solved it.

Did you . . .

      sleep too late?

      forget your ski poles?

      break your ice skate blade?

      get lost on your way to the stadium?

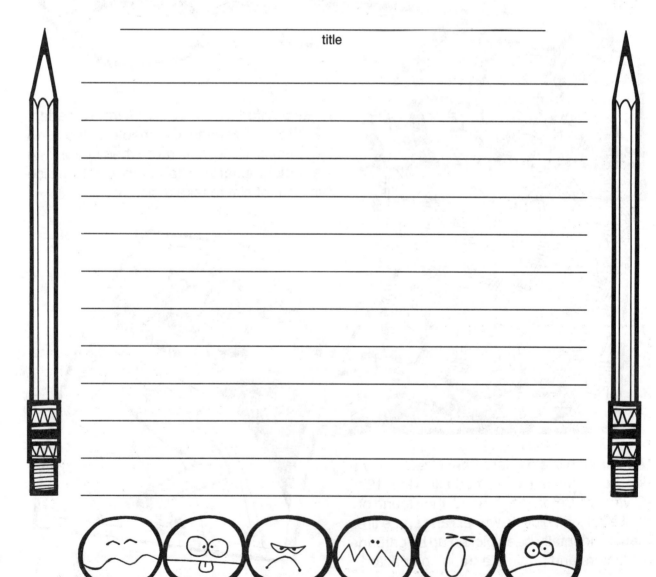

title

Dream On!

Some Olympic athletes dream of success from a very young age.

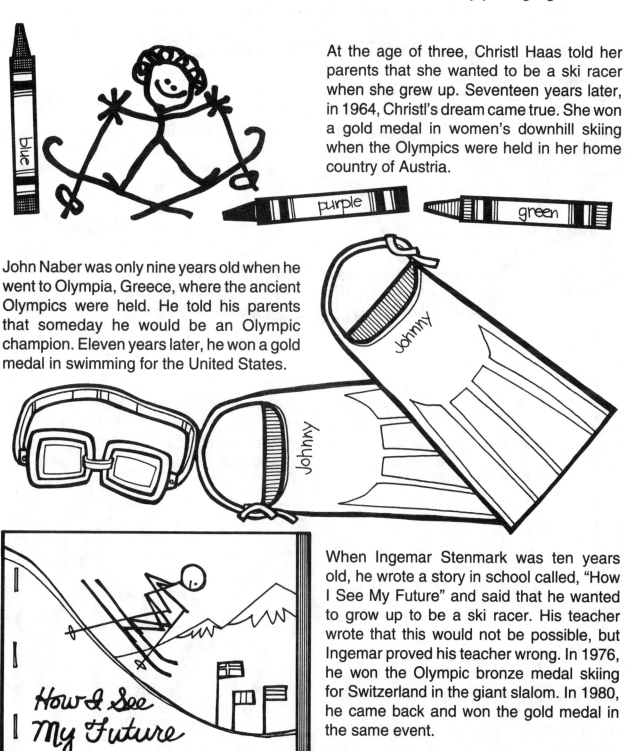

At the age of three, Christl Haas told her parents that she wanted to be a ski racer when she grew up. Seventeen years later, in 1964, Christl's dream came true. She won a gold medal in women's downhill skiing when the Olympics were held in her home country of Austria.

John Naber was only nine years old when he went to Olympia, Greece, where the ancient Olympics were held. He told his parents that someday he would be an Olympic champion. Eleven years later, he won a gold medal in swimming for the United States.

When Ingemar Stenmark was ten years old, he wrote a story in school called, "How I See My Future" and said that he wanted to grow up to be a ski racer. His teacher wrote that this would not be possible, but Ingemar proved his teacher wrong. In 1976, he won the Olympic bronze medal skiing for Switzerland in the giant slalom. In 1980, he came back and won the gold medal in the same event.

Believe It or Not

Sometimes some very strange things happen
at the Olympic Games.

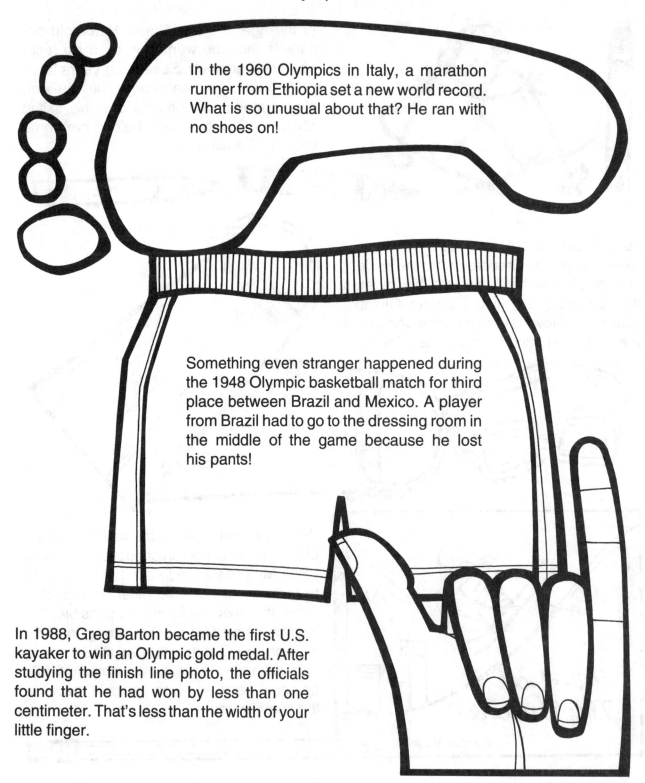

In the 1960 Olympics in Italy, a marathon runner from Ethiopia set a new world record. What is so unusual about that? He ran with no shoes on!

Something even stranger happened during the 1948 Olympic basketball match for third place between Brazil and Mexico. A player from Brazil had to go to the dressing room in the middle of the game because he lost his pants!

In 1988, Greg Barton became the first U.S. kayaker to win an Olympic gold medal. After studying the finish line photo, the officials found that he had won by less than one centimeter. That's less than the width of your little finger.

Believe It or Not!
(continued)

Earl Thomson, a hurdler from Canada, did something very unusual to help get ready for his races. He slept with his feet tied to the foot of his bed so he wouldn't get cramps in his legs. Did it help? He won the gold medal in the 110-meter hurdles in the 1920 Olympics.

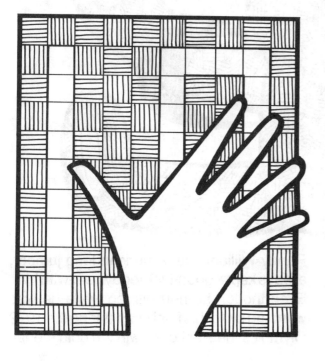

In the 1976 Olympics, Nadia Comaneci from Romania scored the first perfect score in gymnastics history. The scoreboard wasn't designed to flash a score of "10.0" and instead flashed "1.0." A young American gymnast, Mary Lou Retton, watched Nadia's performance on television. Later, when Mary Lou performed on the uneven bars in her first gymnastics competition, she became very excited when the scoreboard flashed "1.0" as her score. Unfortunately, it really was a score of 1.0. Luckily, she did not give up. By the time she performed in the 1984 Olympics, she had earned some perfect scores of her own. Mary Lou Retton became the first American woman to win the all-around gold medal in gymnastics.

Good Luck Charms

No matter how much talent Olympic athletes have, some of them don't take any chances—they remember to pack their favorite good luck charms when they leave home.

George Roth, an American gymnast, was out of work and his family was nearly starving when the 1932 Olympics were held in Los Angeles. He went many days without eating because he could not afford food. He even snuck food from his meals at the Olympic Village and brought it home to his wife and baby. For good luck, he competed with one of his baby's booties stuffed in his shoe. He won the gold medal in club swinging, an event that is no longer part of the Olympics.

Randy Williams, an American long jumper, always kept a good-luck teddy bear with him. Even though he hurt his leg while he was warming up for his final jump during the 1972 Olympics, he went on to win the gold medal.

Good Luck Charms
(continued)

Just before beginning the 1920 long jump competition, William Petterssen of Sweden found a silver coin lying in his path. He picked it up and saw that it was an American coin. He put it in his shoe for good luck and went on to win the gold medal.

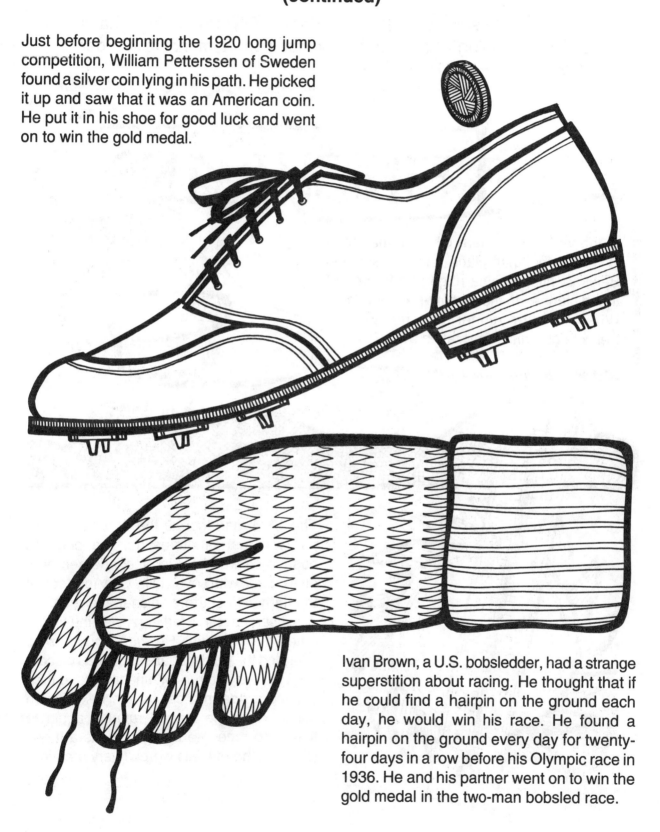

Ivan Brown, a U.S. bobsledder, had a strange superstition about racing. He thought that if he could find a hairpin on the ground each day, he would win his race. He found a hairpin on the ground every day for twenty-four days in a row before his Olympic race in 1936. He and his partner went on to win the gold medal in the two-man bobsled race.

That's Not Fair!

You might be surprised to find that some Olympic athletes have done some things that do not show good sportsmanship in order to try and win a medal.

In the very first modern Olympic marathon in 1896, the third-place winner, Spiridon Belokas, hitched a carriage ride for part of the distance of the twenty-six mile race. When another runner told the judges, Belokas had his award taken away.

The 1904 marathon at the St. Louis Olympics was just as interesting. The long and dusty race was held in ninety-degree heat on a course with seven hills. Only fourteen of the thirty-two starters finished the race. An American runner, Fred Lorz, was the first to enter the stadium. He was about to be awarded the gold medal when it was discovered that he had run for nine miles and then hitched a ride in a car for the next eleven miles before he started running again to finish the race. He thought it was a funny joke, but the officials weren't very amused.

That's Not Fair!
(continued)

Two American brothers won the gold medal in the two-man bobsled run at the 1932 Olympics. They said that part of the reason they won was that they heated the runners of their sled with blowtorches for twenty-five minutes before the race to make their sled go down the track faster. Today they would be disqualified, but they did not break any rules that were in place in 1932. Therefore, the brothers were able to keep their medals.

In the 1984 Olympics, one of the athletes on Puerto Rico's track team hurt her leg in the long jump. Not wanting her team to be left out of the relay race, she asked her twin sister, who was there as a spectator, to take her place in the qualifying run. The coach found out and took his team out of the finals.

Fantastic Olympic Firsts

Number the Olympic events below in the order that they happened. Find the facts you need at the bottom of the page. The first event is numbered for you.

_____ women first competed

_____ first torch relay

_____ Olympic flag first displayed

___1___ first modern Olympics

_____ first Winter Olympics

_____ first women's track and field

_____ only Olympics south of the equator

_____ first Olympics in the United States

- Women first competed in the modern Olympics in 1900.
- The first Olympic torch relay was held in 1936.
- The first time the Olympic flag was displayed was at the 1920 Olympics.
- The first modern Olympics was held in Greece in 1896.
- The first Winter Olympics was held in France in 1924.
- The first track and field events for women were held in 1928.
- The only Olympics held south of the equator was in 1956 in Australia.
- The first Olympics held in the United States was in 1904 in St. Louis, Missouri.

Olympic Crossword Puzzle

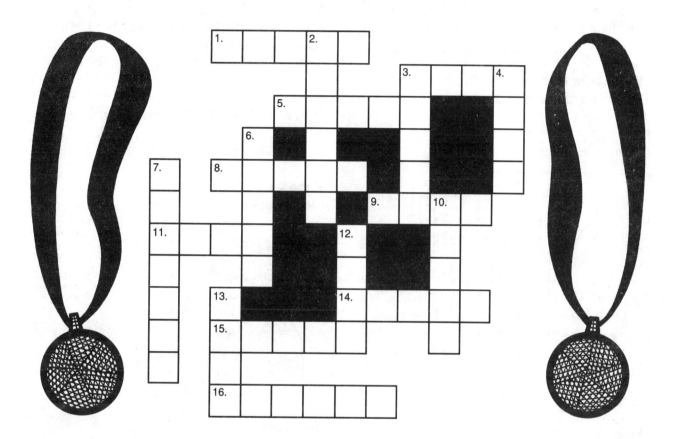

Across:

1. there are five of these on the Olympic flag
3. this flies over the Olympic stadium
5. winners take one home
8. it burns throughout the Olympics
9. gymnasts balance on this
11. parallel and uneven are two types of these
14. this boat's paddle has a blade on *one* end
15. this boat's paddle has a blade on *both* ends
16. ice hockey players wear these on their feet

Down:

2. the first Olympics were held there
3. this burns brightly in the Olympic torch
4. a first-place medal is this color
6. the only animal in the Olympics
7. this sled holds two or four riders
10. this is used with a bow in archery
12. hockey players hit this with their sticks
13. downhill and cross-country are two types

Answer Key

Page 6
A Special Prize
The picture is of a vase.

Page 8
The Chariot Races
The picture is of a chariot.

Page 12
Olympic Word Search

U	V	W	X	Y	Z	A	B	C	F	D	O
N	E	F	G	H	U	N	G	A	R	Y	L
I	J	K	L	M	N	O	R	P	A	A	Y
T	R	S	T	T	U	V	E	X	N	U	M
E	N	G	L	A	N	D	E	Z	C	S	P
D	B	E	C	U	D	E	C	F	E	T	I
S	H	R	I	S	J	N	E	K	L	R	C
T	N	M	O	T	P	M	Q	R	S	A	G
A	U	A	V	R	W	A	X	Y	Z	L	A
T	B	N	C	I	D	R	E	F	G	I	M
E	I	Y	J	A	K	K	L	M	N	A	E
S	W	I	T	Z	E	R	L	A	N	D	S

Page 13
Olympic Events
1. fencing
2. shooting
3. wrestling
4. weight lifting
5. cycling
6. swimming
7. tennis
8. gymnastics
9. track and field

Page 22
Pictogram Match
judo, fencing, weight lifting
canoeing, basketball, archery
gymnastics, diving, swimming
cycling, tennis, boxing
volleyball, hockey, baseball

Page 31
Throwing Events
1. javelin throw
2. discus throw
3. shot put
4. hammer throw

Page 35
Gymnastic Events
men, men, women
both, both, women
men, women, men

Page 40
Summer Sports Match
1. I; 2. B; 3. H; 4. J;
5. E; 6.F; 7. C; 8. A;
9. D; 10. G

Page 42
U.S. Medals in Ten Summer Olympics
1. 1956; 2. 94; 3. 1976;
4. 1964, 1968, 1992; 5. 1992

Page 44
Mogul Maze

Page 62
Fantastic Olympic Firsts
2, 7, 4, 1, 5, 6, 8, 3

Page 63
Olympic Crossword Puzzle